Sir Edmund Hillary

Modern-Day Explorer

Explorers of New Worlds

Sir Edmund Hillary

Modern-Day Explorer

Kristine Brennan

Chelsea House Publishers
Philadelphia

Prepared for Chelsea House Publishers by:
OTTN Publishing, Stockton, N.J.

CHELSEA HOUSE PUBLISHERS
Production Manager: Pamela Loos
Art Director: Sara Davis
Director of Photography: Judy L. Hasday
Managing Editor: James D. Gallagher
Senior Production Editor: J. Christopher Higgins
Series Designer: Keith Trego
Cover Design: Forman Group

First Printing
1 3 5 7 9 8 6 4 2

Library of Congress Cataloging-in-Publication Data

Brennan, Kristine, 1969-
    Sir Edmund Hillary, modern day explorer / Kristine
    Brennan
        p.   cm. – (Explorers of new worlds)
Includes bibliographical references and index.
ISBN 0-7910-5953-7 (hc) – ISBN 0-7910-6163-9 (pbk.)
1. Hillary, Sir Edmund–Juvenile literature. 2. Mountaineers–New Zealand–Biography–Juvenile literature.
[1. Hillary, Sir Edmund. 2. Mountaineers. 3. Mount
Everest Expedition (1953).] I. Title. II. Series.

GV199.92.H54 B74 2001
796.52'2'092–dc21
[B]   00-043077

Contents

The ice-covered peak of Mount Everest, the tallest point in the world, rises more than 29,000 feet above sea level.

On Top of the World   I

At 11:30 in the morning on May 29, 1953, Edmund Hillary and his **Sherpa** guide, Tenzing Norgay, staggered to the top of the world. They had battled exhaustion, winds of up to 100 miles per hour, subzero temperatures, and dangerously high **altitudes** to reach the peak of Mount Everest, the tallest mountain in the world—and the highest place anywhere on earth.

"Nothing above us, a world below," Hillary later wrote in *National Geographic* magazine. He and Norgay were the first people ever to set foot on Everest's frozen summit. Many others had tried to reach the top before them. Since

> **The exact height of Mount Everest is debated. The National Geographic Society lists its height at 29,028 feet. In 1987, using satellite technology, Everest was measured at 29,864 feet.**

1921 at least 16 climbers had died trying and seven expeditions had failed.

One of the first things Edmund Hillary did was take photos of Tenzing Norgay standing on the summit. The pictures would be proof of their achievement. He also carefully photographed the world below from every possible angle.

Hillary and Norgay were taking part in the British Everest Expedition, led by John Hunt. Reaching the summit had required more than two and a half months of nonstop work by an entire team of climbers. The party had packed up some 11 tons of food, tents, oxygen canisters, and other supplies to start their journey. Hunt and his climbers had set up a total of eight camps to travel the final 12,102 feet to the summit.

But as he and Tenzing Norgay stood at the top of Mount Everest, Hillary felt as if the whole adventure had happened to somebody else. "I feel no great elation," he later wrote, "just relief and a sense of wonder." Hillary and Norgay shook hands and hugged.

Norgay was a **Buddhist** and believed that gods lived at the top of Everest, so he buried some small gifts in the snow. Hillary placed a small crucifix next to Norgay's offerings. The two men wasted no time leaving the mountaintop. They were exhausted, and the extreme altitude of Everest was making them weaker with each passing minute. They had to descend safely before they could start celebrating.

The pair dug their ***crampons*** (spiked metal plates attached to boots for climbing in snow or ice) into the steps they had cut with their ice axes on the way up. As they inched down the steep slopes, they were in danger of tumbling headfirst down the mountain. Hillary worried most about a slope of

Everest's most famous victim was a British schoolmaster named George Leigh Mallory. When asked why he wanted to climb Mount Everest, he answered, "Because it is there." In June 1924 Mallory and his partner, Andrew Irvine, disappeared into the mist surrounding Everest's north face and never came back down. Mallory's body would remain hidden in the snow near the summit until 1999. To this day, some believe that Mallory scaled Everest before Hillary and Norgay.

Edmund Hillary (left) and Tenzing Norgay relax after conquering Everest. Word that men had finally reached the highest point in the world made the two climbers international heroes overnight.

soft, slippery snow that led to a drop down into the Kangshung Glacier. "If one of us begins to slide, both of us will enjoy a 10,000-foot jump without benefit of a parachute," he later joked.

After gingerly making their way down what Hillary described as a "glassy staircase," the men faced only one remaining enemy: exhaustion. George Lowe, a strong climber who had been key to paving the way for Hillary and Norgay, greeted them with steaming tomato soup and extra oxygen. He was first to hear their good news. Other expedition members awaited word in lower-altitude camps, but Everest's conquerors would spend the night high up in Camp VIII. Once Lowe led them there, Hillary and Norgay crept into their sleeping bags and tried to sleep despite their excitement.

The morning of May 29, 1953, marked Edmund Hillary's transformation from an adventurous 33-year-old beekeeper to a genuine hero. Word of Hillary and Norgay's amazing climb reached England on June 1, the night before the coronation of young Queen Elizabeth II. She would soon make Edmund Hillary a Knight of the British Empire. He would barely shake Everest's snow off his boots before beginning a whirlwind lecture tour. This former "restless, rather lonely child" was now a man admired by millions.

But Edmund Hillary was not finished living out his boyhood dreams of adventure. His successful climb to the top of Everest was just one of the "firsts" that Edmund Hillary would accomplish. Adventure would lure him across Antarctica, up one of India's most sacred rivers—and to the misty peaks of many mountains to come. As a boy he had read about other people's daring deeds; from now on, his own adventures would spark the world's imagination.

Edmund Hillary was born in New Zealand, an island in the South Pacific near Australia that is part of the British Commonwealth.

From Daydreams to Reality

2

$\mathcal{E}$dmund Percival Hillary was born in Auckland, New Zealand, on July 20, 1919. Edmund, his older sister June, and younger brother Rex grew up in the small town of Tuakau with strict parents.

Edmund admired his father's strong character. The elder Hillary worked as the reporter, editor, and printer of the *Tuakau District News*. After a disagreement with his bosses, he gave up the newspaper and turned his small beekeeping business into a full-time job. Edmund and his brother Rex started tending the beehives as young boys. They enjoyed the vigorous outdoor work.

Edmund's mother was a schoolteacher who tutored him at home. He zipped through lessons so quickly that he was ready for high school two years early. It took two hours to get to the high school by train, so Edmund read to pass the time. He could finish an entire book on most days. He especially liked adventure books. "I died dramatically on a score of battlefields and rescued a hundred lovely maidens," he later said about his vivid imagination.

Despite his love of reading, Hillary was not a particularly good student in high school. His first two years were hard, partly because he was so much younger than his classmates and did not have many friends. Edmund eventually caught up to his class-mates physically, reaching an impressive six feet, three inches in height. By the time he was 16 years old he had grown strong and confident. He took a rare vacation from the bee business during winter break from high school to go on a ski trip to Mount Ruapehu, an active volcano in New Zealand.

After his high school graduation, Edmund enrolled in Auckland University. Hillary did not make many friends at the university. Instead, he filled his spare time with his favorite books and out-door activities. He dropped out after two years and began working full time with his father's beekeeping business.

When New Zealand entered World War II, Edmund Hillary did not have to join the military, because beekeepers, like other types of farmers, were needed to produce food. Despite this, he joined the Royal New Zealand Air Force. He worked as a navigator doing search and rescue over the Pacific Ocean.

Edmund Hillary walked in snow for the first time on his high school ski trip to Mount Ruapehu. As he skied and explored the mountain on foot, Hillary felt freer and more alive than ever before–even enjoying the cold! "I soon developed a taste for the mountains that has never left me," he later wrote.

After the war ended, Edmund Hillary's adventures were just beginning. He resumed beekeeping with his father, but spent his free time climbing New Zealand's mountains. Within a few years Edmund and Rex took over the beekeeping business. But Edmund's love of climbing was opening a whole new way of life to him.

Mountain climbing even led him to his future wife. Hillary was friends with Jim Rose, who was president of the New Zealand Alpine Club. Jim's daughter, Louise, a music student, wasn't fond of risky climbing, but she was a strong, energetic person. She caught Edmund Hillary's eye as she slid down a mountain! Louise had come with Hillary and a few friends for a practice climb on Mount Ruapehu. As Hillary stood below the climbers and coached them, he was startled to see Louise speeding down an icy slope. When she finally landed at the bottom, Hillary went to see if she was all right. "I rushed down to join her and she lay smiling up at me, bruised but undamaged. . . . I determined that I would get to know her better," he remembered.

In 1951, Hillary and two other climbers visited Garhwal, India, to climb in the **Himalayas** for the first time. Hillary and his companions spent several weeks exploring these mountains between India and Tibet. While Hillary and these other climbers were still exploring India, they received a message from Eric Shipton, an Englishman who was organizing an expedition to the south side of Mount Everest to find a route to the top. Could two of them join his climbing party in Nepal immediately?

Hillary later described the opportunity as "the sort of chance you could only dream about." He and fellow New Zealander Earle Riddiford scrambled to gather supplies. They traveled by train, by canoe, and on foot to catch up with Shipton and the rest of his party in the town of Dingla, Nepal.

At first, Hillary doubted that they would find a way up the south side of Mount Everest. Most climbers had attempted to scale the north face, located in Tibet, which was considered easier to climb than the south side. However, foreigners were not allowed in Tibet after 1951, when the country was taken over by communist China. So Eric Shipton and his party really had no choice but to search for a route on the south face.

Although he was not optimistic about the outcome of the trip, Hillary jumped at the chance to climb with Shipton, whom he idolized. But the expedition to the south face yielded a surprise. Together, Hillary and Shipton reached an altitude of 19,000 feet. At that height, they spotted a possible path the rest of the way up Everest.

They knew that the route would be very difficult and dangerous, but they believed that it was worth a try. Staging an attack on Mount Everest would take months of planning and preparation. It would also take a group of strong and nearly fearless climbers.

"Get up
If You Can"

A climber scales the dangerous Khumbu Icefall on Everest. One slip here and the climber could drop 10,000 feet. (Inset) John Hunt, who replaced Eric Shipton as leader of the 1953 British Everest Expedition.

3

In 1952, climbers from Switzerland made two attempts on Mount Everest. Edmund Hillary and his fellow climbers feared that the Swiss would scale the summit first. But Swiss mountaineer Raymond Lambert and guide Tenzing Norgay didn't quite make it on the first try. They reached about 28,000 feet, but retreated after a brutal night in a tent with no sleeping bags. The Swiss climbers tried again in the fall; again, Everest won.

Although Hillary admired their brave attempt, he longed for his own chance to climb Everest. But soon after he was invited to join the 1953 British Everest Expedition, Hillary learned that a 42-year-old World War II hero named John Hunt had replaced Eric Shipton as the leader.

Hillary and a fellow New Zealander named George Lowe met the rest of the British party in Katmandu, the capital city of Nepal. They also met Tenzing Norgay, the Sherpa *sirdar* (leader), who brought a crew of mountaineers. Some would haul supplies to set up camps, one would cook for the expedition, and the strongest climbers would take part in the high-altitude ascent.

Tenzing Norgay was to accompany the party only as far as his health permitted. This would be the 39-year-old Sherpa's sixth journey up Everest. He had made his first attempt in 1935 as a young ***porter***; more recently he had accompanied Lambert in

The Sherpa people were originally from Tibet, but they migrated to Nepal and parts of India hundreds of years ago. Life in the Himalayan foothills meant that the Sherpas were used to high altitudes. Most lived as farmers, yak herders, or traders.

Tenzing Norgay, a Sherpa, was an experienced climber. He had accompanied Swiss mountaineer Raymond Lambert in two failed 1952 attempts to scale Everest. Norgay was the leader of the Sherpas employed by the British Everest Expedition to carry supplies and help with the assault on Everest.

1952. The Swiss expedition had taken such a toll on Tenzing's strength, however, that he doubted his ability to go for the summit again so soon.

He had good reason to feel doubt. Everest can kill even the strongest climbers. The climbing season is only in late spring or during the fall. In winter, high winds would blow climbers right off the mountain; in summer, Everest's loosely packed snowdrifts lead to avalanches. Temperatures can dip as low as −40 degrees Fahrenheit, while winds can reach speeds of 100 miles per hour. Some called Everest earth's "third pole"–as hostile to human exploration as the North Pole and Antarctica.

Europeans named the highest mountain in the world after a British surveyor, Sir George Everest. However, the people of Tibet, who live in the shadow of the mountain's north side, call it *Chomolungma*, or "Goddess Mother of the World." Everest's south side is in Nepal, whose people call it *Sagarmatha*, or "Churning Stick of the Ocean of Life."

Everest's fierce conditions were foremost in John Hunt's mind as he planned the expedition. He spent months arranging the transport of food, supplies, and tents. Hunt brought oxygen devices that would help the climbers to breathe as they neared the summit. At high altitudes, air contains very little oxygen. This means that a climber, who is already working hard, must breathe much faster and more deeply than normal to survive. His or her body also has to produce extra red blood cells to carry oxygen through the body more efficiently. That is why people must do high-altitude climbs very carefully and gradually. If a climber ascends a mountain before his or her body adjusts to the lack of oxygen, unconsciousness and death will occur in minutes.

The oxygen sets made for Hunt's team reduced the risks of climbing higher than 20,000 feet. They weighed roughly 30 pounds and used replaceable oxygen canisters. However, the air hoses and masks sometimes froze, cutting off the oxygen supply.

Before Hunt's party could attack Everest, however, they had some 175 miles of walking to do. They made their official start on March 10, 1953. Hillary and the others appreciated the 17 days of walking through Nepal and into the foothills of Everest. They slowly got adjusted to high altitudes as they approached the mountain.

Rear Camp was their final stop before the climbing really began. The party set up this campsite on the grounds of a *monastery* in Tengboche, Nepal. The Buddhist monks there ran a wildlife refuge. Hillary and his companions watched animals and birds wander around their tents as they tried to organize their supplies for the trek to Base Camp, which would be nearly 17,000 feet up the mountain. They also staged a few practice climbs and taught the Sherpas how to use their oxygen sets. Only the most skillful of Tenzing Norgay's Sherpas were still with the team at this point, and they all needed oxygen sets to make high climbs with Hunt's team.

Before the British climbers started their ascent, the *abbot* of the Tengboche monastery warned them to watch out for **yetis**, or abominable snowmen. He said that yetis were apelike creatures about five feet tall and covered with reddish hair!

If there were any yetis on Everest, they would have seen a busy stream of expedition members and Sherpas carrying heavy packs up their mountain. Although only two climbers would eventually reach the summit, getting them there would take a great effort from everyone. The team set up progressively higher camps as they got closer to the top. John Hunt sent pairs or small groups of climbers ahead while the rest stayed at camp. These advance climbers left tracks in the snow, hacked steps in the ice, and secured rope ladders to help the next group of climbers. The lower camps were supply stations and rest stops for climbers about to advance on Everest's peak. One group climbed to a higher level, then dropped tents and supplies for the next group before heading back down. The expedition worked this way because climbers could not carry tents and supplies up the mountain, and then have enough strength left to continue going higher. Hunt's party operated like relay racers, with everyone climbing his leg of the journey to position the strongest, fittest climbers near the top. If even one person stood on

The monastery at Tengboche is nestled in the foothills of Everest. It was at this Buddhist sanctuary that the British expedition prepared to ascend the mountain.

Everest's summit, then everyone would share in the expedition's success.

After Base Camp, the British Everest Expedition set up seven more campsites as climbers moved up the mountain. Progress was not easy, however. They faced dangers like the Khumbu Icefall, a terrifying expanse full of huge chunks of moving ice. The icefall, which sits below the Khumbu Glacier, is also covered with **crevasses** deep enough to swallow a climber whole. The icefall was so steep that Hillary and the others could only screw ropes into solid ice and hope for the best as they inched upwards. "It was exciting climbing," wrote Hillary, "and always underneath we had a feeling of tension and danger." According to John Hunt, his party had to abandon Camp II, located in the icefall, because of "alarming glacial movements."

But the expedition's most serious work began once they reached Camp IV, or Advance Base Camp (21,200 feet). It was now mid-May, and the daily snowfalls on Everest could undo a day's work without warning. Nothing was more discouraging than cutting steps in the ice all afternoon, only to see them buried in fresh snow the next morning. But the team persevered, setting up a camp in the Western Cwm ("koom"), a small valley above the Khumbu Glacier (22,000 feet). From there, the only way to reach the South Col (25,800 feet) was to go partway up nearby Lhotse (a mountain peak standing 27,890 feet high). On May 21, Wilfrid Noyce and a Sherpa named Annullu were the first climbers to reach the South Col—an altitude of nearly 26,000 feet! Hillary and Tenzing reached the South Col soon after the first climbers.

Edmund Hillary and Tenzing were ready to gun for the summit. John Hunt decided that to save food and supplies, only those directly involved in the final assault on Everest should remain at Camp VIII. In addition to Hillary and Tenzing, George Lowe, Alf Gregory, and Sherpas Ang Nyima and Pemba would stay. Before departing for a lower camp, Hunt reminded Hillary that safety mattered most. "But," he added, "get up if you can."

But Pemba could climb no higher: vomiting from altitude sickness, he stayed behind. The rest of the party picked up an unassembled tent and supplies left by Hunt at 27,500 feet. Hillary noticed that Ang Nyima was also getting sick and needed to go lower to recover. But after the Sherpa headed down the mountain, along with Alf Gregory and George Lowe, he and Tenzing felt very much alone.

First, they had to claw into the frozen ground to make a flat place for their tent. After putting it up, they tried to rest in preparation for the next day's climb. But Hillary spent much of the night keeping the tent from blowing away in the howling wind. It was also so cold (-17°F in the morning) that Hillary's boots were frozen. He had to warm them on the stove until they were soft enough to wear.

Everest's strong winds buffeted Edmund and Tenzing's tent. "When I hear [the wind] whistle on the ridge," Hillary later wrote, "I brace myself against the canvas and try to hold the tent down as it gets ready to take off."

The snow near the summit was powdery. This required extra caution. As he moved through the soft, unpacked snow, Hillary knew he was at risk of being caught "aboard an avalanche with a one-way ticket to the bottom." In icy spots, he and Tenzing had to take turns chopping footholds into the mountain with ice axes and then using climbing ropes to help each other up the sheer slopes.

The most difficult obstacle was "a ghastly great rock about 40 feet high" that blocked their way to the top. Hillary decided to take a potentially deadly gamble. There was a ***cornice*** (a mass of ice and snow hanging over a ledge) on the rock's right side. Hillary stuffed his lanky frame into the space between the rock and the cornice, and then inched up to the top of the rock. The effect was something like climbing up a chimney—except that he risked falling thousands of feet to certain death. "My tactics depend on one little consideration: that the cornice doesn't peel off," he later quipped.

Although he estimated that the crack was only about 40 feet long, Hillary says that it took him at least half an hour to climb up it. After collapsing at the top to catch his breath, he passed down a rope to Tenzing. It wasn't until they were both safely over the giant rock that Edmund Hillary truly believed that they would make it.

Still, Hillary momentarily doubted that he would ever find Everest's summit as he steadily chopped steps into the ice. But he soon looked up and saw that there was nothing left to climb! His memories of that moment in his book, *Ascent*, are surprisingly low-key. "I chipped steps over bump after bump, wondering a little desperately where the top could be. . . . A few more whacks with my ice-axe and Tenzing and I stood on top of Everest."

The members of the British Everest Expedition are welcomed on their arrival in England. In the front, from left, are Edmund Hillary, Tenzing Norgay, John Hunt, and George Lowe.

From Beekeeper to Hero

4

At 11:30 A.M. on May 29, 1953, Edmund Percival Hillary became a real-life hero. He carefully snapped pictures of everything in sight to prove that he and Tenzing had been atop Everest. But Hillary did not show Tenzing how to use the camera, so there are no pictures of him on the summit. "I knew I'd been there, and that was good enough for me," he later explained.

Hillary and Norgay were exhausted and their oxygen supply was dwindling, so they started their descent. The rest of the team was waiting for the good news, but they still had to get down safely from the earth's highest point.

As they passed the "dismal little campsite" where they had spent the previous night, Hillary and Norgay spotted George Lowe climbing up to greet them. He was carrying hot tomato soup and extra oxygen. Edmund flashed Lowe a smile and confirmed that they had "knocked the blighter off."

The climbers were too tired to say much more. They hobbled into camp on the South Col. "We crawl into our sleeping bags with a sigh of sheer delight," Hillary later wrote. But excitement made it hard for them to sleep. The next day, they joined up with the other expedition members. The entire party then headed down the mountain for the march back to Katmandu.

On the way down Everest, they stopped at the monastery in Tengboche to thank the abbot for his prayers. But the abbot was not convinced that Hillary and Norgay had reached the summit, because they hadn't seen the gods who lived there!

The king of Nepal was more impressed with the British Everest Expedition than were the monks of Tengboche. The climbers were honored guests in the king's court at Katmandu. But the adventurers were not exactly dressed to visit royalty: they donned outfits ranging from shorts and sneakers to pajamas!

Queen Elizabeth II, shown in a portrait made on her coronation day, received a special gift the night before she was crowned—word that British climbers had succeeded in reaching the world's highest point.

News of the expedition's success didn't reach England until late on June 1—the night before the **coronation** of young Queen Elizabeth II. Before Hillary returned home to New Zealand, he and the other members of the British Everest Expedition visited Buckingham Palace. There, the new queen knighted Hillary and Hunt. From then on, the world would know the shy beekeeper from Auckland as Sir Edmund Hillary.

America also honored the first successful Everest expedition. On February 11, 1954, Hillary and Hunt met with President Dwight D. Eisenhower to receive the National Geographic Society's gold Hubbard

Tenzing Norgay was not knighted; he received the Empire Medal instead. Although England slighted Norgay's achievement, he became a hero both in Nepal, his birthplace, and in India, his adopted homeland.

Medal on behalf of the entire expedition team.

During the year following his triumph on Everest, Sir Edmund Hillary gave lectures throughout the world. At least he had company, though. Before Everest, Edmund Hillary and Louise Rose had talked about marriage. After his triumphant return, Louise left Sydney, Australia, where she was studying music, and returned to Auckland. On September 3, 1953, the couple became Sir Edmund and Lady Louise Hillary. Sir Edmund treasured Louise's company when he traveled, later calling their marriage the happiest 22 years of his life.

But when he returned to Auckland in February 1954, Sir Edmund had less than six weeks to set up a home with his wife before going back to the Himalayas. On March 28, 1954, Hillary assembled a party of 10 climbers and a team of Sherpas. He wanted to explore Baruntse, a 23,570-foot peak. Another goal was to find a way up Makalu, an unclimbed Himalayan mountain 27,790 feet high.

Sir Edmund and Lady Louise Hillary walk through an arch of ice axes after their wedding. They were married on September 3, 1953, in Auckland, New Zealand.

The party succeeded in finding a possible route up Makalu, although they did not reach the top. They did, however, scale 23 other Himalayan peaks before anyone else. Although all were smaller than Everest, Hillary found them just as challenging.

One interesting aspect of Hillary's 1954 expedition had nothing to do with climbing. Charles Evans photographed two sets of mysterious footprints in the snow. They were human-like, except for claw marks where the toes should have been. Had a pair of yetis passed through the area before the climbers?

The 1954 expedition was not without its problems, though. Hillary collapsed at high altitude on a climb. He blamed the collapse on three broken ribs that made breathing difficult. He had broken his ribs while trying to rescue a fellow climber, Jim McFarlane, who had fallen into a deep crevasse. McFarlane was trapped overnight. He lost all of his toes and two of his fingers to frostbite.

When Sir Edmund Hillary returned home, he and Louise started their family with the birth of their son, Peter. A daughter, Sarah, soon followed. Even though he could scale Mount Everest—and almost any other mountain in the world—at times Hillary found parenthood even more challenging.

His restless spirit soon took him away from home again. He jumped at the chance to go to the South Pole when British geologist Vivian Fuchs asked for his help. Fuchs wanted to cross the entire continent of Antarctica, something no one had ever done before.

Fuchs knew that a single party could not carry enough supplies, food, and fuel for the entire 2,158-mile trek across this dangerous continent, where temperatures could dip below -60°F. Fuchs needed a support party from New Zealand to set up five supply stations for the last 700 miles of his journey. Sir Edmund couldn't resist the invitation to head this team, although he felt guilty about leaving his family behind for such a long time. It would take 16 months to complete his leg of the expedition.

At the end of 1955, Hillary joined Fuchs to help set up a base camp on the Weddell Sea side of Antarctica. But their boat got trapped in ice, stranding them until January 30, 1956. They frantically unloaded their supplies and left Fuchs's team to build a base before departing. Hillary and his party set sail for McMurdo Sound, on the other side of Antarctica. The New Zealand crew was responsible for stocking Scott Base—Fuchs's final destination—

with supplies. They would then head for the South Pole. Along the way, they would establish five more supply depots for Fuchs's party to use on their way to Scott Base. Hillary would take a route to the South Pole that nobody else had ever tried.

On October 14, 1957, Hillary's team began their overland trek to the South Pole. They used British-made farm tractors fitted with crawler tracks over the wheels to keep them from sinking in the snow. The tractors were the best mode of transportation that anyone could think of. They sometimes fell into crevasses that were hidden beneath the snow. Their drivers were shaken but unhurt when this happened; the real problem was towing the tractors out of the crevasses.

Sometimes, the blinding snow made it hard for Hillary to tell if he was going in the right direction. Compasses were no help: the magnetic South Pole causes compass needles to point downwards and stay there. This is because the force of the earth's rotation is so strong at both the North and South Poles that it creates a magnetic field. Hillary was forced to rely on a **sextant**, an instrument that tells users where they are by measuring the angle between the earth's horizon and the stars.

One of the modified tractors, known as "Sno-Cats," that Hillary and Fuchs used to cross Antarctica. The Sno-Cats had a top speed of about four miles per hour.

Progress was slow, and they had to stop frequently to repair their vehicles. Hillary was embarrassed when the New Zealand party covered just six miles on the first day. He could still see Scott Base from his campsite! It often felt as if they would never succeed in setting up the supply depots. But they persevered, finishing the job on December 20, 1957.

Although the New Zealand team had succeeded in setting up the depots for Fuchs, Sir Edmund was not satisfied. He wanted to get to the South Pole! His team left their extra gear behind and continued

Sir Edmund Hillary (second from right) stands with some of the members of the New Zealand team that reached the South Pole in January 1958.

toward the Pole. On January 4, 1958, Sir Edmund Hillary achieved another "first": the New Zealand Party became the first to reach the South Pole using overland motor vehicles. Hillary had led his team a total of 1,250 miles. He was still there when Fuchs and his team reached the South Pole 15 days later.

Fuchs was knighted after his trek across Antarctica. His team had made many important scientific discoveries. For example, they found plant fossils many millions of years old that showed that Antarctica once had a tropical climate.

For the next two years, Hillary concentrated on his family and his beehives. He and Louise welcomed their third child, Belinda. But his serene life at home would not last for long. The publishers of *World Book Encyclopedia* agreed to fund another Himalayan expedition. This time, Hillary had multiple goals. His party would attempt to climb Makalu without oxygen to help scientists study the body's adjustment to high altitudes. Hillary also wanted to build a school for Sherpa children in the village of Khumjung, Nepal. In addition, the expedition would search for proof of the yeti's existence.

Hillary did not reach the top of Makalu—without oxygen, altitude sickness forced him to turn back at 23,000 feet. And although expedition members did find tracks in the snow, they found no other evidence of yetis. However, in 1961 Hillary and three other expedition members built a school for the Sherpa village of Khumjung.

Hillary wanted to repay the Sherpas who had climbed with him for their courage and loyalty, so building schools for them became one of his top priorities. A whole new life was beginning for him and his family—a life that would bring both joys and sorrows he never dreamed possible.

Testing the Water

5

The Khumjung School was made of aluminum sheeting carried piece by piece to the site. Hillary wanted the villagers to know that the school was truly theirs, not just a gift from an outsider, so he made sure that its construction was a joint effort between his party and the community. A Sherpa teacher named Tem Dorje became the Khumjung School's first headmaster when the school officially opened on June 12, 1961.

Sir Edmund Hillary founded The Himalayan Trust, an organization that raises money for building projects in the Solu Khumbu region of Nepal. By the start of the year 2000, the trust had built 27 schools, two hospitals, and 12 clinics, as well as numerous bridges and water systems.

By this time, Hillary's expeditions and *humanitarian work* had ended his beekeeping career. He was now a professional adventurer and aid worker. Like today's sports stars, Hillary had *endorsement deals*. After his yeti-hunting expedition to the Himalayas, he spent a year lecturing in America for the publishers of *World Book Encyclopedia*, who had funded his climb.

Sir Edmund moved his family to Chicago for the year while he gave lectures to fulfill his contract. In the summer of 1962, the Hillarys went to Alaska with a film crew in tow: this time, Sir Edmund was working as an expert spokesman for Sears Roebuck and Company's camping equipment.

But he always went back to the mountains he loved. In 1963, he set off with a carefully selected party for the Himalayan Schoolhouse Expedition. Hillary and his charitable organization, The Himalayan Trust, were flooded with requests from

Sherpa leaders seeking schools for their children. On this trip, he wanted to build schools in Thami and Pangboche, two villages close to Khumjung. In Khumjung, Hillary wanted to set up a medical clinic and to increase the Sherpas' water supply. He also wanted to set up a better water system in nearby Khunde. As if this were not enough, Hillary also planned to do some climbing: his party would attack the peaks of Taweche and Kangtega, both

A Sherpa teacher instructs a village class at the Khumjung School, one of many that The Himalayan Trust has helped build in the past 30 years.

over 20,000 feet high. Hillary did not actually do any of the climbing on these mountains, but he was very proud of his team, which just missed the top of Taweche by about 200 feet. His climbers had better luck on Kangtega. After setting off on May 29, 1963—the 10th anniversary of Hillary and Tenzing's Everest victory—they reached the summit.

But the expedition's most important work was entirely unplanned. **Smallpox** was spreading through the region. Hillary saw its effects firsthand in a small village, and he arranged for donations of vaccine. When it arrived, expedition doctor Phil Houghton taught several other expedition members how to immunize the Sherpas against smallpox. Although they could not save everyone from the disease, Hillary later estimated that they vaccinated more than 7,000 people.

By 1975, aid work was so important to the Hillary family that they were spending the year in Katmandu.

> **"Of all the programs we carried out on the expedition—schools, waterworks, medical clinics, and the like—the one most widely appreciated was undoubtedly the [smallpox] vaccination, and this hadn't been part of my original plans,"** Hillary later wrote.

Peter was now a young man, Sarah was a university student, and 16-year-old Belinda was taking correspondence courses. Sir Edmund could travel easily from their rented house in Katmandu to work on his aid projects in the Solu Khumbu region.

Flying to and from the mountains was not without risk, however. On the morning of March 31, 1975, the plane carrying Louise and Belinda crashed on the way to the town of Paphlu, where they were to join Sir Edmund in dedicating a hospital being built by The Himalayan Trust. At 9 A.M., a helicopter landed where Hillary was waiting. A friend got out and sadly informed him that his wife and daughter had been killed. Although he was nearly overwhelmed with grief, he took it upon himself to tell Louise's parents, who were also waiting for her. He asked the helicopter pilot to fly him to the crash site. He had to see the wreckage for himself.

Hillary soon went back to work on the hospital in Paphlu, trying his best to keep busy. Sometimes, he would take lonely walks in the airfield he'd made near the construction site. "In the evening I walked alone on the airfield with the great mountains behind—and my sorrow seemed to ease a little—or at least nobody could see my tears," he wrote in *Ascent*.

This wreckage is from the plane crash that killed Sir
Edmund Hillary's wife Louise and daughter Belinda.
The explorer was devastated by their deaths.

On May 1, 1976, the Solu Hospital officially opened
in Paphlu. Although he was pleased with his work,
the completion of the hospital left him sadly wondering what to do next.

Sir Edmund Hillary found his answer in the summer of 1977. That was when he also found himself
headed up India's most sacred river in a jet boat. He
had assembled a party of 19 to attempt the first boat
trip up the Ganges River. He called this expedition
Ocean to Sky. On August 24, three jet boats—the

Ganga, the *Air India*, and the *Kiwi*—began their journey in the Bay of Bengal, heading past many holy cities along the banks of India's sacred river. When the boats could go no farther, the crew would walk into the town of Badrinath. From there, the party would climb a Himalayan mountain. Sir Edmund's son, Peter, now 22 years old, would be one of the mountaineers leading the way to the top. Hillary had some old Sherpa friends with him, including Mingma Tsering, who had been part of the Everest expedition. "The journey would be full of excitement and variety, and have its share of danger, too—what more could one ask than that?" Hillary wrote.

On the waters of the Ganges, Hillary and his party faced many dangers. The boats sometimes ran aground on sand bars at the bottom of the river, which caused many cuts and bruises. The party was warned to beware of crocodiles and tigers. Hillary and his team saw both.

> Hillary had dreamed of testing the waters of the Ganges for a long time. It took years to get India's permission to conduct the expedition and to make a film of it. Despite the red tape, the Indian people welcomed Hillary's party at every city along the river.

As they moved into the final stages of their battle against the Ganges River currents, Hillary also battled self-doubt. The crew was facing dangerous rapids that could easily overturn the jet boats and sink them rapidly. "It worried me sometimes that I might kill off some of my friends with my crazy ideas," he wrote. But then he reminded himself that he had never lost a life on any of his expeditions.

In fact, Hillary and his crew helped save a life during Ocean to Sky. Near the town of Viyasi, they had stopped after *Air India* nearly sank in a rapid. Someone noticed a "small bundle of rags" across the river: it turned out to be an old man who had tumbled to the bottom of a steep riverbank. Unable to climb back up to his walking trail, the man had gone without food for two weeks before the *Ganga*'s crew drove across the river and carried him to safety.

When the Ocean to Sky party approached the town of Nandaprayag, a waterfall 10 feet high blocked the boats' way. It was impossible to drive them any further. They had traveled 1,500 miles upriver on the jet boats—a first.

Now it was time to head for the sky on foot. The party was reduced to 10 climbers. They had about 100 miles to walk before they reached the mountain they would climb: Akash Parbat, which stood over 19,000 feet high.

The climb went well for the 58-year-old Hillary until the party reached High Camp at 18,000 feet. On the morning of October 14, Sir Edmund did not wake up. Expedition doctor Mike Gill tried to shake Hillary awake. Gill knew that their leader was gravely ill with altitude sickness. The climbers joined forces to get Hillary down to safety.

Since he was unconscious in his tent, they had to collapse it with him still inside and drag it over the frozen ground. It was difficult and dangerous work. Peter Hillary was among those working to pull his father to safety. Their hard work was not in vain. They stopped at 15,500 feet, where Hillary got better rapidly. On October 15, a helicopter flew him to a hospital, where he spent two days undergoing tests. While he was gone, his climbers scaled Akash Parbat.

After completing Ocean to Sky, Hillary returned to Katmandu. He was horrified to see how many juniper trees had been cleared in Nepal, leaving behind bare wasteland. He still mourned his wife and youngest daughter. He also sadly realized that he was no longer young and strong. Could Sir Edmund Hillary bounce back from his grief?

HEARTY WELCOME TO SIR EDMUND HILLARY AND O
HAPPY REUNION IN NEPAL ON THE OCCASION OF
F THE HISTORICAL CONQUEST OF MOUNT EVER

"More a Beginning than an End"

Sir Edmund Hillary (front, right) and other members of the 1953 Everest expedition met in 1993 to celebrate the 40th anniversary of their historic climb. Even at more than 80 years old, Hillary often visits Sherpa villages in the Himalayas and remains active in humanitarian work.

6

*I*n a 1999 interview, Hillary remarked, "Everest for me was more a beginning than an end." His life had become proof of his words. He kept on adventuring after reaching an age when many people think about retiring.

In 1981, the 62-year-old mountaineer joined an expedition in search of a climbing route up the north (Tibetan) side of Mount Everest. This time, younger climbers would go for the summit: Hillary was there to advise them. The expedition members met in Lhasa, Tibet, where Hillary visited with his old friend, Tenzing Norgay. Tenzing—a living legend in the Himalayan region— was still strong and fit at 66.

The party started trekking on August 20. By September 1, altitude sickness took its toll on Hillary. Expedition doctor Jim Morrissey accompanied him a couple thousand feet lower as he moved from Base Camp to Yak Camp. Hillary recovered and returned to Base Camp—only to suffer from confusion, headaches, and vomiting. On September 14, Morrissey started taking Hillary all the way down the mountain. Along the way, the oxygen-starved Hillary mistook a big rock for a truck coming to rescue him. A startled yak also knocked him into some boulders, opening a wound in his head. Dr. Morrissey treated the cut and helped him to safety.

The other climbers had not been very lucky either. Heavy, soft snow forced them to stop more than 7,000 feet below the summit. Hillary decided that his "big mountain days" had come to an end.

In September of 1982, Sir Edmund Hillary did something unusual. He visited India just to look around and enjoy the view. For once, he was not fund-raising, organizing, or following a schedule to beat dangerous weather conditions. He walked the beaches of Bombay and visited holy temples; he rode in a taxicab instead of a jet boat.

In February 1985, Hillary returned to India when he became New Zealand's high commissioner to that country. While in office, one of his top priorities was opposing the deforestation of land in India and Nepal. He held this position until 1989.

By this time, Sir Edmund was no longer alone. His new wife was June Mulgrew, the widow of a fellow climber named Peter Mulgrew. In 1979, Peter Mulgrew had taken Sir Edmund's place as a guide on a tourist flight over Antarctica. Tragically, the plane carrying Mulgrew slammed into a mountain. Sir Edmund Hillary and June Mulgrew—friends for about 20 years—comforted each other on their mutual losses. They were companions for many years, and married in November 1989.

During Hillary's term as high commissioner to India, he visited his friend Tenzing Norgay several times. Sir Edmund last saw his old friend alive in 1986; on May 9 of that year, Norgay died at age 71.

Hillary was 66 years old at the time of Tenzing Norgay's death. His days in the Himalayas were far from over, however. Instead of exploring, though,

Sir Edmund Hillary continued to dedicate himself to helping the Sherpas. Hillary personally helped to build many of the schools and hospitals. The schools were his way of showing his concern and affection for Sherpa children. "They had bare feet and scruffy clothes," Hillary remembers about the first 40 pupils of one school, "but their rosy cheeks and sparkling eyes were irresistible." With education, these children could choose careers other than yak herding, and dream of the world beyond their villages.

Hillary does not feel that everything he has done is positive. In 1964, he built an airfield to help bring in building materials and supplies, but it also brought in tourists. Soon, climbers and trekkers were using tons of firewood for heating and cooking. Hillary was already concerned about the Sherpas' heavy harvesting of trees; when outsiders started using wood, too, the problem got worse. Today, The Himalayan Trust does reforestation work to replant trees in the Khumbu region.

In 1998, the Smithsonian Institution honored Sir Edmund for his tireless aid work. The Smithsonian presented Hillary with a James Smithson Bicentennial Medal in honor of his efforts in Nepal. "There is so much [that needs to be done], really, that it's impossible for us to deal with it all," Hillary says of the number of requests for help he gets.

Although his schedule no longer includes mountain climbing, Hillary still visits his Sherpa friends, reaching villages in the Himalayan foothills by helicopter rather than by foot.

More than 800 people have climbed Everest to date, because Sir Edmund paved the way. But Mount Everest is now covered with permanent ropes and ladders to help tourists, who pay tens of thousands of dollars for guided climbs to the top.

Sometimes, the tourism boom on Everest makes people forget how dangerous the mountain still is. Even today roughly one out of every 30 climbers still dies on the way up, and of those who do get to the top, one out of every four doesn't reach the bottom alive. In 1996, an expedition that included Tenzing Norgay's son, Jamling Tenzing Norgay, successfully followed Hillary and Norgay's 1953 route up the mountain's south side. They were shooting a film of their climb, but on May 10 they had to stop their work to help with a massive rescue effort. Climbers from three other expeditions were also on the mountain, and many became trapped at high altitude during a sudden storm. Eight climbers died. Sir

Two great mountaineers: Sir Edmund Hillary and Reinhold Messner, an Austrian who in 1978 became the first man to climb Mount Everest without using oxygen.

Edmund has since spoken of his belief that inexperienced climbers have no business on Everest.

In May 1999, Sir Edmund Hillary was disgusted by the behavior of two American mountaineers who found and photographed George Mallory's long-lost body. Many people still believe that Mallory, a British mountaineer who attempted to reach the summit of Everest in 1924, actually succeeded but died on his way back down. This would make Hillary the second person to scale the mountain. When a photograph of Mallory's body—frozen for 75 years at high altitude—appeared in print, Hillary lashed out at the media for publishing it. He believed that George Mallory's body should have been treated with more respect.

Hillary also says that if anyone ever found proof that Mallory scaled Everest first, he would not be upset. This is because fame has never gone to his head. "I do not take it seriously. . . . If someone wants to believe that I'm a heroic figure, fine, but for me, I did a reasonable job at the time. I didn't get carried away then, and I never have."

Hillary's face appears on New Zealand's five-dollar bill, but his mind is on helping others. He could have turned his hero image into a life of wealth and luxury, but he used it to raise public awareness of people in need. Sir Edmund Hillary climbed Mount Everest, became a knight, and lived a life of constant adventure because he never stopped trying to overcome his own limitations. When he met with incredible success, he decided to share it with the Sherpa people of Nepal.

Today, Sir Edmund Hillary still lives bravely and generously. As he grows older, his adventurous spirit remains vital. "I'm a little slower than I used to be," he said recently, "but I hope to be going as long as I possibly can."

His many admirers share his hope.

Chronology

1919 Edmund Percival Hillary is born in Auckland, New Zealand, on July 20.

1951 Climbs in the Himalayan Mountains for the first time; joins Eric Shipton in search of a route up Mount Everest.

1953 Joins British Everest Expedition, led by John Hunt; with Tenzing Norgay, reaches the top of Mount Everest on the morning of May 29; is knighted by Queen Elizabeth II; marries Louise Rose.

1954 Receives Hubbard Medal from the National Geographic Society; organizes climbing party in the Himalayas that scales 23 previously unclimbed mountains.

1955– Participates in Vivian Fuchs's expedition across Antarctica;
1958 on January 4, 1958, leads crew to the South Pole, becoming the first to reach it in overland mechanical vehicles.

1961 Builds first school, in the Sherpa village of Khumjung.

1963 Organizes the Himalayan Schoolhouse Expedition to build schools, water systems, and medical clinics; vaccinates 7,000 Sherpas for smallpox.

1975 Wife Louise and daughter Belinda are killed in a plane crash on March 31.

1977 As director of the Ocean to Sky expedition, explores the Ganges River for 1,500 miles, then climbs Akash Parbat.

1985 Becomes New Zealand's high commissioner to India, a post he holds until 1989.

1989 Marries longtime companion June Mulgrew.

1998 Honored by the Smithsonian Institution for aid work.

abbot—the person in charge of a monastery.

altitude—elevation above a given level (usually sea level).

Buddhist—a person who follows the teachings of Buddha. These teachings, called Buddhism, make up the chief religion of Asia.

cornice—a mass of ice and snow hanging over a mountain ledge.

coronation—the crowning of a sovereign.

crampons—spiked metal plates attached to boots for climbing in snow or ice.

crevasse—a deep, open chasm in a glacier.

endorsement deals—arrangements in which a famous person is paid to promote a particular product.

humanitarian work—charity work, or projects that are done solely for the benefit of others.

Himalayas—a mountain range in Asia that includes some of the highest peaks in the world.

monastery—a settlement of people (often called monks) who have dedicated themselves to religion.

porter—a person employed to carry equipment or supplies on an expedition.

sextant—an instrument that uses the stars to measure distances and directions.

Sherpa—a group of people living in Nepal and parts of India.

smallpox—a sometimes-deadly infectious disease, caused by a virus, that can be prevented through vaccination.

yeti—a creature believed to live in the Himalayas.

Further Reading

Deford, Frank. "Our Favorite Feats." *Sports Illustrated*, 27 December 1999.

Friend, Tim. "Sir Edmund on Top of the World in Life of Service." *USA Today*, 17 November 1998.

Fuchs, Sir Vivian. "The Crossing of Antarctica." *National Geographic*, January 1959.

Herrick, Stefan. "A Mountain of a Man." *The* (Wellington, New Zealand) *Evening Post*, 17 July 1999.

Hillary, Sir Edmund. *Schoolhouse in the Clouds*. Garden City, N.Y.: Doubleday, 1964.

———. *Nothing Venture, Nothing Win*. New York: Coward, McCann and Geoghegan, 1975.

———. *From the Ocean to the Sky*. New York: Viking Press, 1979.

———. "Preserving a Mountain Heritage." *National Geographic*, June 1982.

———. *View from the Summit*. Auckland, New Zealand: Doubleday, 1999.

Hillary, Sir Edmund, and Peter Hillary. *Ascent*. Garden City, N.Y.: Doubleday, 1986.

Hunt, Brigadier Sir John, C.B.E., D.S.O. "Triumph on Everest: I. Siege and Assault." *National Geographic*, July 1954.

Krakauer, Jon. *Into Thin Air*. New York: Villard, 1997.

Voboril, Mary. "The Top of the World." *Newsday*, 14 May 1997.

Index

Picture Credits

KRISTINE BRENNAN has written several books for Chelsea House, including a biography of Lady Diana Spencer and a history of the Stock Market Crash of 1929. She and her husband live in Newtown Square, Pennsylvania, with their two children.